Published in 2025
by Two Windmills Limited

Marine House, Tide Mill Way,
Woodbridge, Suffolk, IP12 1AP
United Kingdom

www.twowindmills.com

A CIP catalogue record for this book is available from the British Library.

ISBN 978-1-83555-371-8

Printed in Guangdong, China
10 9 8 7 6 5 4 3 2 1

SURVIVAL 101

EXTREME EDITION

Written by Nat Lambert
& Mike Jarmain

CONTENTS

KANSAS
MISSOURI
OKLAHOMA
Wichita
Kansas City
Topeka
Salina
Hutchinson
Smoky Hills
Red Hills
Springfield
Tulsa
Oklahoma City
Grand Island
Lincoln
Concordia
Garden City
Scott City
Ness City
Jefferson City
Columbia
120
140
160
180
SE
S

WELCOME TO SURVIVAL 101!

Do you have what it takes to face the wild, outsmart danger, and explore the unknown? This book is here to teach you amazing survival skills that will make you feel like a true adventurer!

Whether you're braving the backyard, exploring the wilderness, preparing for extreme situations, or imagining supernatural challenges, you'll learn how to handle tricky situations with courage and smarts.

There are four survival levels to master in this book. If you take time to learn the skills, then **this book could save your life!**

EXPERT SURVIVAL TIP

Remember—safety comes first. These survival techniques in this book are for fun and learning, and you should only try them with the help of an adult or qualified outdoor survival guide.

SPECIAL-ISSUE KEYCHAIN: YOUR ULTIMATE SURVIVAL SIDEKICK

A **paracord keychain compass** is more than just a cool accessory—it's a survival tool packed with practical uses for adventurers of all kinds. Whether you're hiking, camping, exploring, or tackling a backyard survival challenge, here's why this handy gadget is a must-have survival sidekick for any young adventurer.

PARACORD: KEYCHAIN FOR THE OUTDOORS

The keychain is made from strong paracord that is designed for outdoor survival.

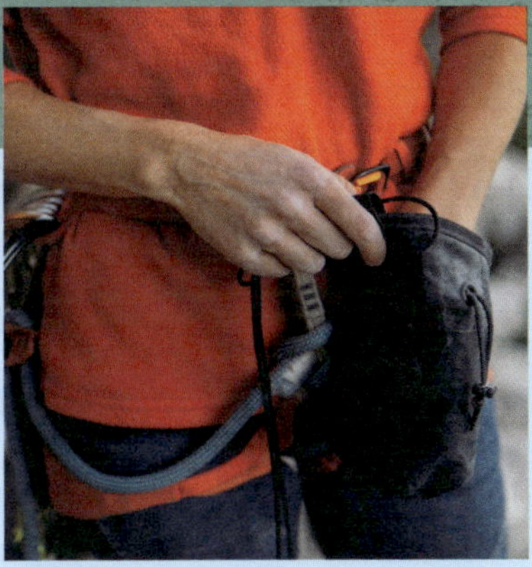

Carrying gear. The cord is strong enough to secure items to your backpack or hang food out of reach of animals.

Signal for help. If you're stranded, use the compass as a reflective surface to catch the sunlight and signal to rescuers (see Morse code on pages 34-39).

COMPASS: NAVIGATE LIKE A PRO

The built-in compass ensures you never lose your sense of direction!

Find your way. Use the compass to navigate toward safety if you get lost (see pages 24-25).

Plan your path. Combine the compass with a map to stay on track during hikes.

> "Study nature, love nature, stay close to nature. It will never fail you."
>
> Frank Lloyd Wright

LEVEL 1 »

BACKYARD SURVIVAL

BACKYARD SURVIVAL

Start your survival training close to home! Learn about essential kit, how to navigate by the stars, use a compass, basic first aid, and much more!

These skills are great for camping trips, vacations, and summer camp. Who knew you could practice survival without ever leaving your neighborhood?

ESSENTIAL SURVIVAL SAFETY KIT

When you're heading out on an adventure—whether it's a backyard campout or a big hike—it's important to have the right gear to keep you safe and prepared. A survival safety kit is like your superhero utility belt, filled with tools that can help in tricky situations. Here's what you should know about building and using one.

THE ESSENTIALS FOR EVERY KIT

These items are must-haves for staying safe and solving problems.

Water bottle and purification tablets. Staying hydrated is priority number one, and these tools help ensure your water is clean and safe.

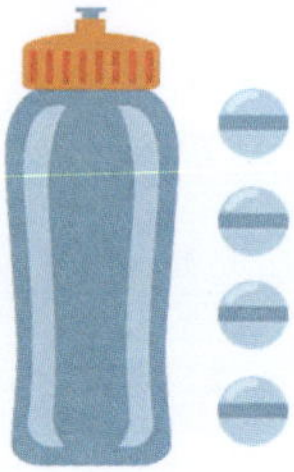

Snacks. Pack high-energy foods like granola bars, nuts, or dried fruit to keep your energy up.

First-aid kit. Include bandages, antiseptic wipes, and tweezers for treating cuts, scrapes, or splinters.

Whistle. A loud whistle can help rescuers find you if you're lost. Three short blasts is the universal signal for help.

Flashlight or headlamp. When the sun goes down, this will light your way (don't forget extra batteries!).

TOOLS FOR ADVENTURE

These items come in handy for exploring and problem-solving:

Multi-tool or pocketknife. Perfect for cutting rope, sharpening sticks, or opening a snack (use with an adult's help!).

Compass and map. These are lifesavers if you're exploring a new area. You've got a compass on your special-issue keychain.

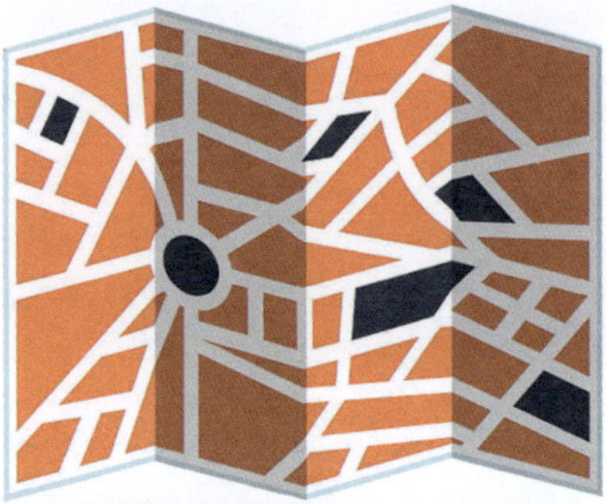

Paracord keychain. As we learned earlier, this tool has lots of important survival uses.

Firestarter. Matches, a lighter, or a flint and steel can help you make a fire to stay warm or cook food.

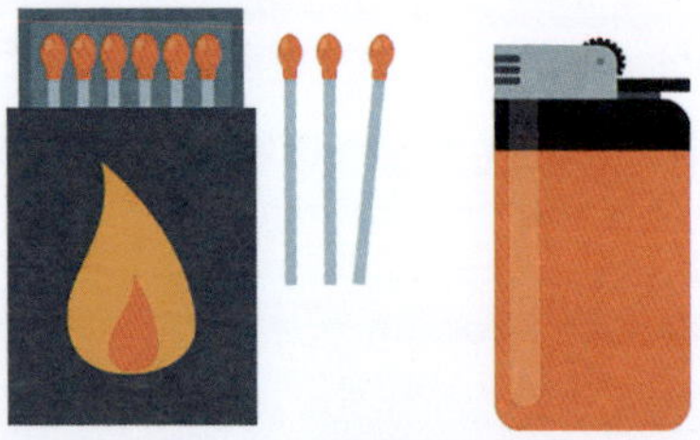

STAYING COMFORTABLE

Rain poncho. Stay dry and cozy, even if the weather surprises you.

Warm hat and gloves. Even summer nights can get chilly, especially in the wild.

Emergency blanket. These super-thin blankets trap heat and keep you warm in a pinch.

EXPERT SURVIVAL TIP

Your survival safety kit is your trusty sidekick, but the smartest tool you have is your brain. Stay calm, think things through, and use your kit to help you stay safe on your adventures!

> “You can be a hero by learning and providing first aid when the time comes.”
>
> Red Cross

BASIC FIRST AID FOR OUTDOOR ADVENTURES

Accidents can happen when you're out exploring, but knowing a few simple first-aid tips can really help to save the day! With these skills, you'll be ready to handle small problems and help keep everyone safe. Remember—always call for an adult if someone is seriously hurt.

SMALL CUTS AND SCRAPES 101

Wash your hands (or use hand sanitizer) to keep germs away.

Clean the cut with clean water or an antiseptic wipe.

Gently pat it dry and cover it with a bandage or band aid to keep it clean.

EXPERT SURVIVAL TIP

If you don't have a bandage, use a clean piece of cloth or tissue.

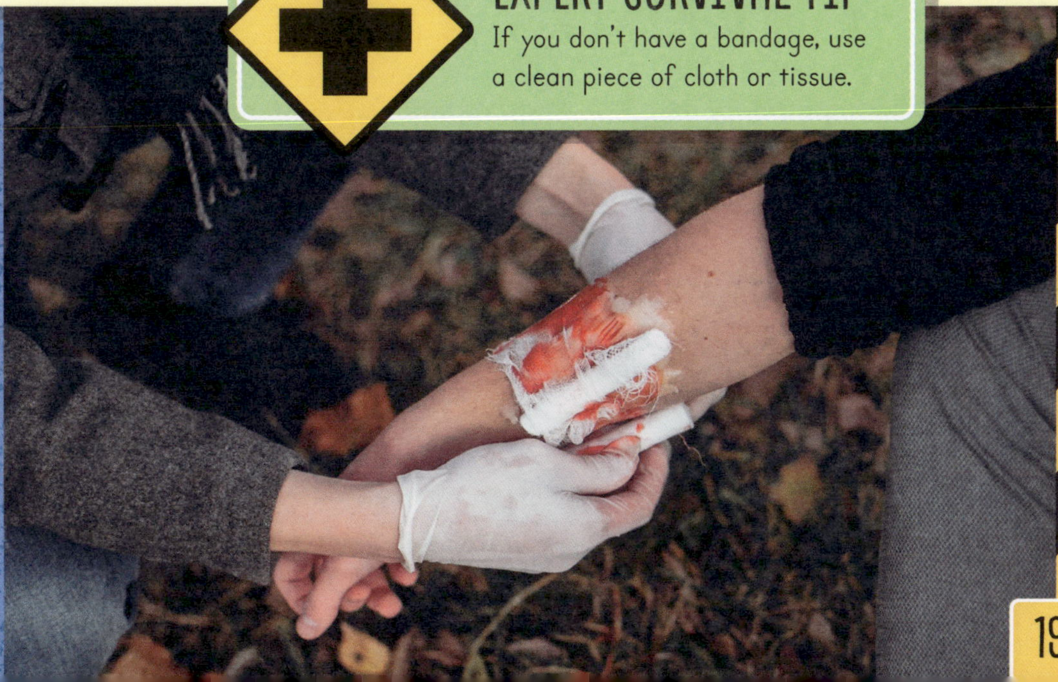

HELPING A NOSEBLEED 101

Sit down and lean forward slightly. Pinch the soft part of your nose with your fingers and hold it for 10 minutes.

Keep calm and don't tilt your head back—this can make blood go down your throat.

EXPERT SURVIVAL TIP

If the bleeding doesn't stop after 10 minutes, seek medical assistance.

WHAT TO DO FOR A BURN 101

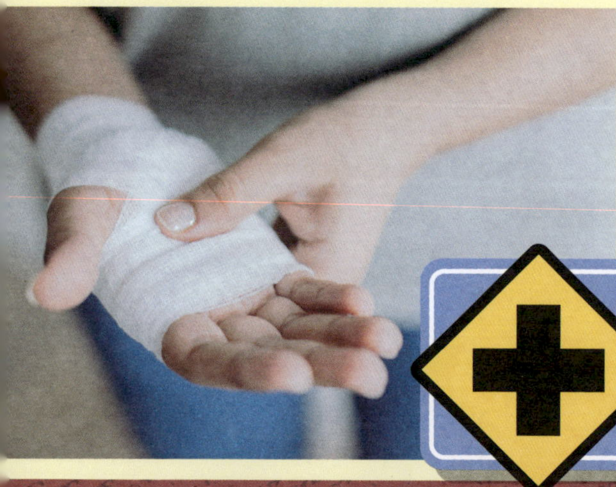

Cool it down if it's a small burn. Run cool water over it for at least 10 minutes.

Don't pop any blisters—they help protect the skin underneath.

Cover the burn with a clean, loose cloth or bandage.

EXPERT SURVIVAL TIP

For bigger burns, seek medical assistance right away.

SPLINTER REMOVAL 101

Wash your hands and the area with the splinter. Make sure it's completely clean.

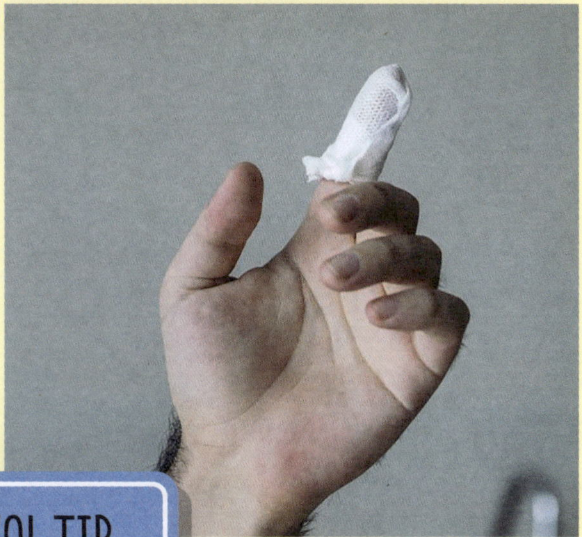

Use tweezers to gently pull the splinter out.

Clean the area again and cover it with a bandage if needed.

EXPERT SURVIVAL TIP

If the splinter is too deep or won't come out, seek medical assistance.

BEE STING 101

EXPERT SURVIVAL TIP

Bee stings hurt, but staying calm helps you handle it better.

Remove the stinger by scraping it off gently with a card (like a credit card).

Wash the area with clean, cool water.

Apply a cold cloth or ice pack to reduce swelling.

If the person feels sick or has trouble breathing, seek medical assistance immediately!

WHAT TO DO IF SOMEONE FAINTS

Lay the person flat on their back and make sure their legs are slightly raised.

Make sure the area around them is safe. Try not to move the person after placing them in the correct position.

Call for an adult or emergency help immediately. It's important that the person gets professional help quickly.

EXPERT SURVIVAL TIP

Don't try to move someone who has fainted unless they're in danger.

FIRST-AID KIT CHECKLIST

Here are a few items every explorer should have in their first-aid kit.

- Bandages (different sizes) and Band-Aids
- Antiseptic wipes
- Tweezers
- Gloves
- Small scissors
- Painkillers (always follow medicine directions for use).

Remember, being calm, careful, and confident is the best first-aid skill you can have. With practice and the help of an adult, you'll be ready to handle small emergencies like a true survival expert!

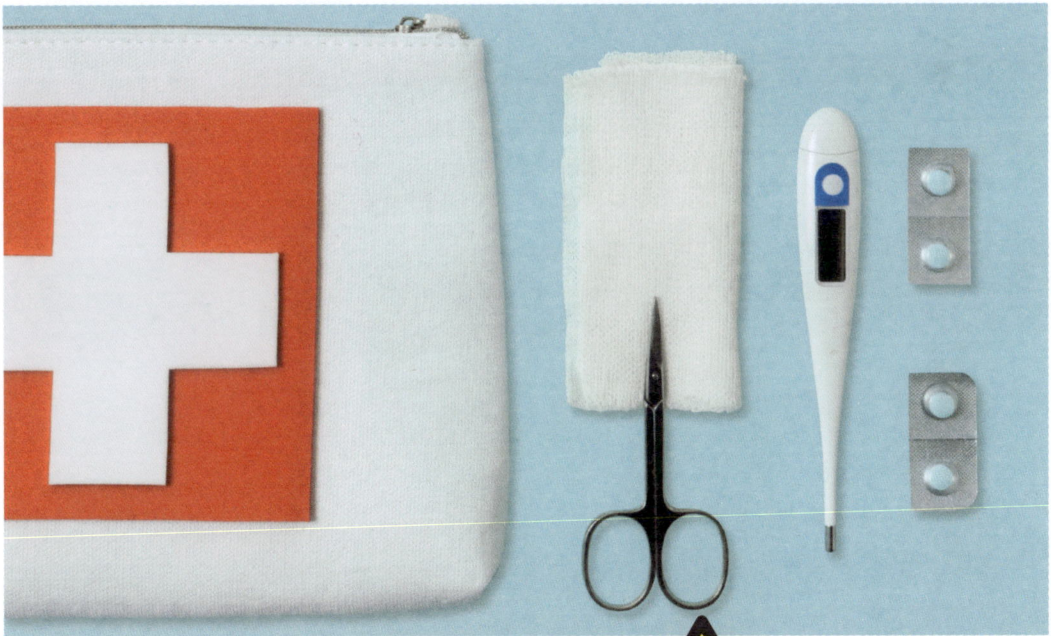

WHEN TO GET IMMEDIATE HELP

If someone has trouble breathing, is bleeding a lot, or isn't waking up, call for help immediately! If there isn't an adult to help you, dial 911 for assistance.

HOW TO USE A COMPASS: A QUICK GUIDE FOR ADVENTURERS

The compass on your paracord keychain is a simple but powerful tool that helps you find your way in the great outdoors. It's like a little magic arrow that always points to north! Here's how to use it.

GET TO KNOW YOUR COMPASS

The compass dial features easy-to-follow markings for north, east, south, west, as well as northeast, southeast, southwest, and northwest.

EXPERT SURVIVAL TIP

Avoid metal objects. They can make the compass act funny.

FIND NORTH 101

Hold the compass flat in your hand so the floating circular dial can spin freely.

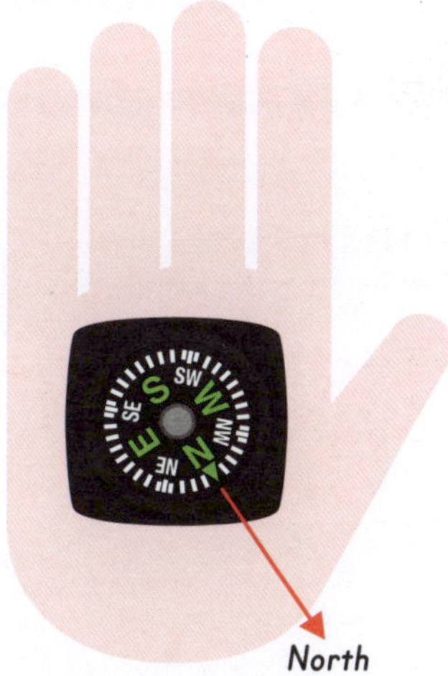

Wait for the dial to settle, then look at where the N with the arrow points. That's north! All the other bearings (S, W, E) will also be pointing the right way.

PLOT A ROUTE

Ask an adult to help you to research the direction of a friend or relative's house that is in your neighborhood. See if you can follow the compass bearing to reach your destination. For example, grandma's house is one block away to the southeast.

With a little practice, your compass will be your trusted guide, helping you explore the world with confidence!

EXPERT SURVIVAL TIP

Practice makes perfect. Mark out the compass bearing of key locations (park, grocery store, etc.) from your house and see if your friends or family can use the compass to find them.

Stars are much easier to see in the wilderness. Light pollution in cities can make them much more difficult to spot.

NAVIGATE USING THE STARS

There are millions upon millions of stars in the night sky, but they aren't just beautiful—they can help you find your way at night! Here's a super-simple way to use the stars for navigation.

FIND THE NORTH STAR (POLARIS) IN THE NORTHERN HEMISPHERE

- Look for the **"Big Dipper"**—a group of stars shaped like a big spoon.
- Find the two stars at the edge of the "bowl" of the Big Dipper. The stars we are interested in are called Dubhe **(x)** and Merak **(y)**.
- Draw an imaginary line from those two stars, going upward—they'll point straight to the **North Star** (Polaris), which is marked **"z."**
- The North Star always points to **north,** so if you face it, you know:
- **North is in front of you.**
- **South is behind you.**
- **East is to your right.**
- **West is to your left.**

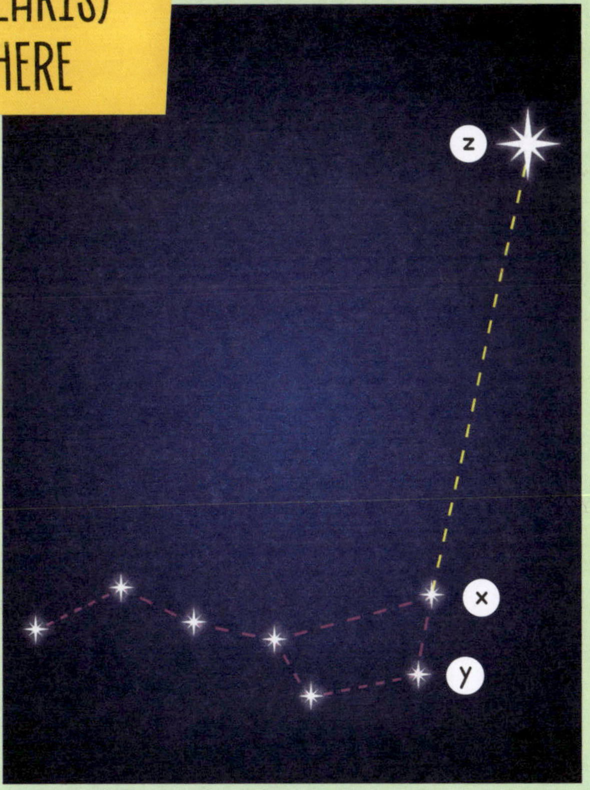

See if you can pick out more star constellations in the night sky using the charts on the next pages.

CONSTELLATIONS 101: THE NORTHERN HEMISPHERE

The northern star constellations can be observed in the Northern Hemisphere, located to the north of the equator.

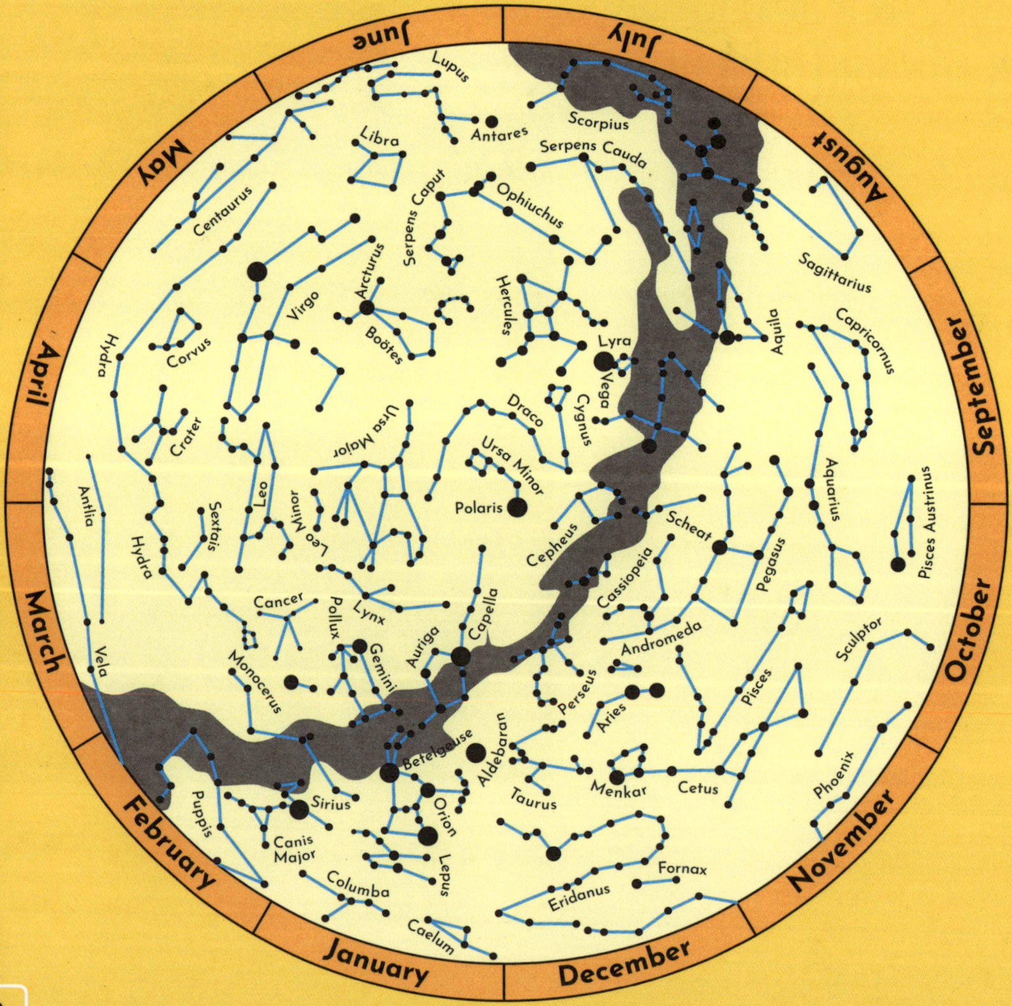

"I know the stars are my home. I learned about them, needed them for survival in terms of navigation. I know where I am when I look up at the sky."

Gene Cernan

CONSTELLATIONS 101: THE SOUTHERN HEMISPHERE

The southern star constellations can be observed in the Southern Hemisphere, located to the south of the equator.

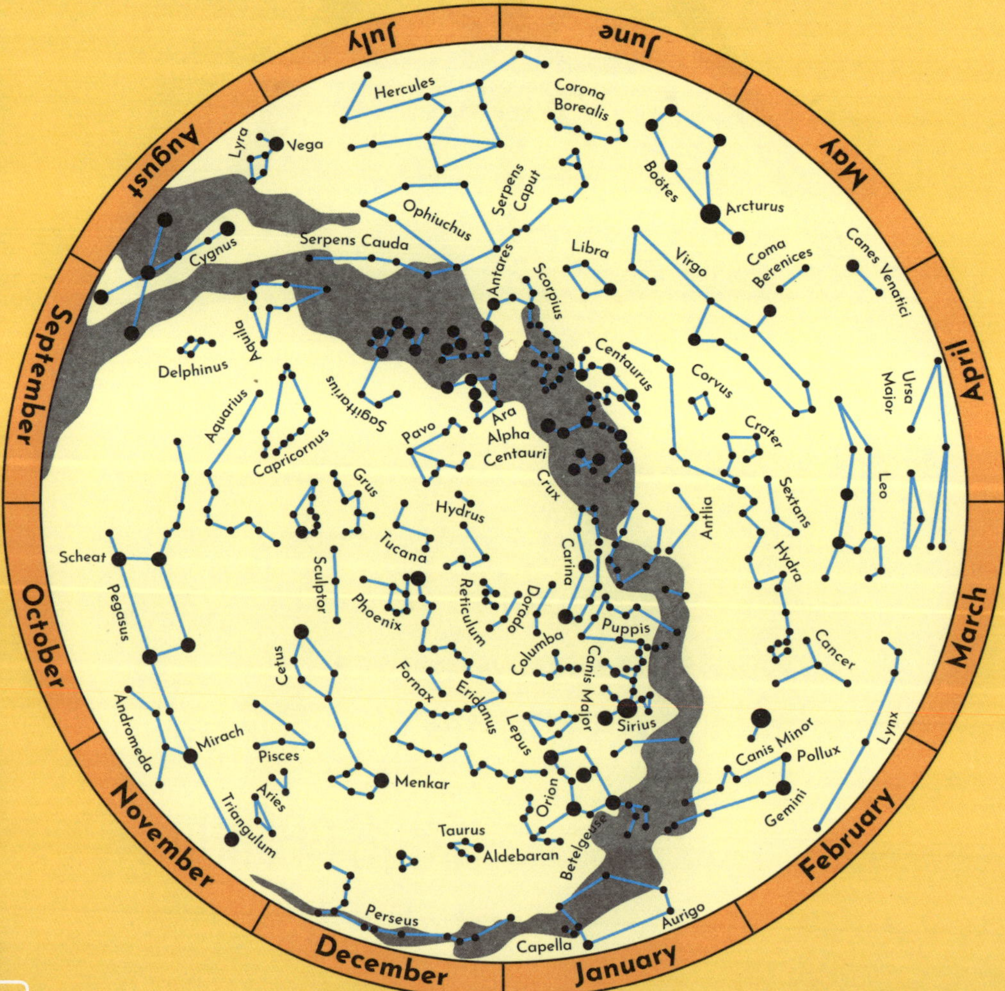

“Set your course by the stars, and not by the light of every passing ship.”

Omar Bradley

NATURAL NAVIGATION

During the daytime, try these two great methods for working out directions. They both use the sun and so you will need to try them on a day when it's not too cloudy!

USING THE SUN 101

Sailors have been using the sun to help them navigate for centuries—and now you can, too!

The sun is very useful as an aid to direction. Every day, it rises in the east and sets in the west.

At midday in the Northern Hemisphere, the sun is always due south. At midday in the Southern Hemisphere, the sun is due north.

The sun rises in the east.

The sun sets in the west.

SHADOW CLOCK 101

Did you know that you can use shadows to accurately work out direction?

1. Find a patch of clear space and stick a straight pole, about 3 ft. long, into the ground.

2. Use a twig to mark where the tip of the shadow falls.

3. Wait about 15-20 minutes and mark where the tip of the shadow has moved to.

4. The first mark will be **west,** and the second will be **east.** By placing your left foot by the first mark and your right foot by the second mark, you will now be facing **north**—amazing!

MORSE CODE SOS!

Morse code is like a secret language made of dots (short sounds or flashes) and dashes (long sounds or flashes). It's a great way to send messages when you're in trouble, especially if you don't have a phone with you.

LEARN THE SOS SIGNAL

The most important Morse code message to know is **SOS,** which means "I need help!" It's easy to remember.

Dot-dot-dot (S): 3 short signals

Dash-dash-dash (O): 3 long signals

Dot-dot-dot (S): 3 short signals again

In total, it looks like this:

• • • — — — • • •

WAYS TO SEND A MORSE CODE SOS

You can use lots of things to send Morse code:

Flashing lights: Use a flashlight or your phone.

Tapping or knocking:

- Clap or tap on a tree or a metal surface.
- Tap or clap quickly for dots.
- Tap or clap slower and longer for dashes.

Whistling: Use short and long whistles in the SOS pattern.

WHEN TO USE MORSE CODE

- If you're lost and need rescuers to find you.
- If you see a plane or helicopter, flash the SOS signal toward them.
- If you're out at sea on a life raft and need to catch the attention of a passing ship.

PRACTICE AT HOME

- Try sending the SOS signal with a flashlight.
- Ask a friend or family member to guess what you're signaling. You might need to give them the Morse code 101 key, pictured on pages 38–39, to do this!
- See how quickly you can do it!

WHY MORSE CODE WORKS...

Rescuers know to watch and listen for Morse code signals, especially SOS. Even if you can't talk or use a phone, Morse code can get their attention and bring help your way.

Now you're ready to communicate like a survival pro!

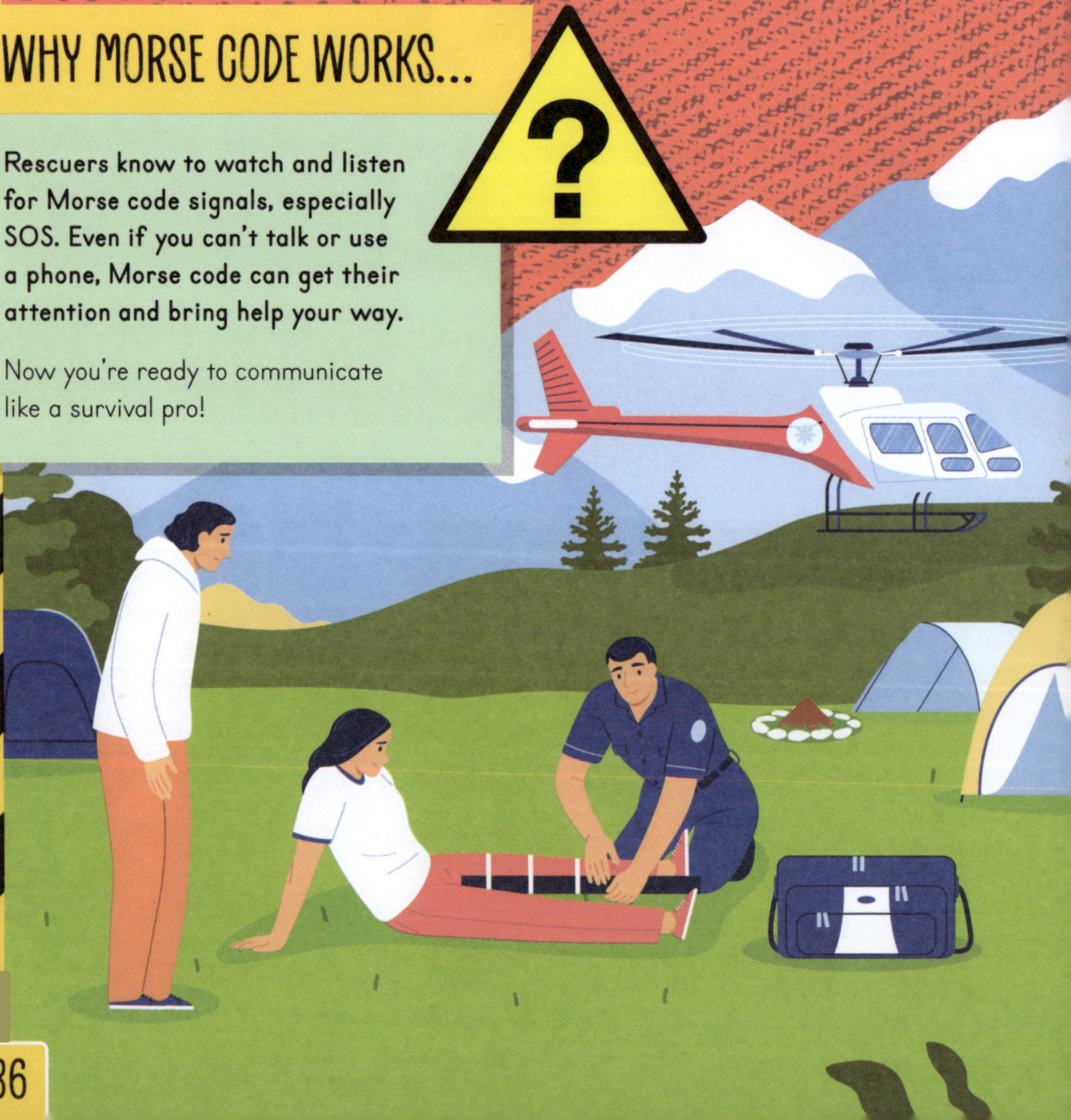

The first Morse code message was sent on May 24, 1844, by Samuel Morse. Morse sent the bible quote "what hath God wrought?" by telegraph from Washington D.C. to Baltimore.

MORSE CODE 101

A ·–

B –···

C –·–·

D –··

E ·

F ··–·

G ––·

H ····

I ··

J ·–––

K –·–

L ·–··

M ––

N –·

O –––

P ·––·

Q ––·–

R ·–·

S ···

T –

U ··–

V ···–

W ·––

X –··–

Y –·––

Z ––··

Full stop ·–·–·–

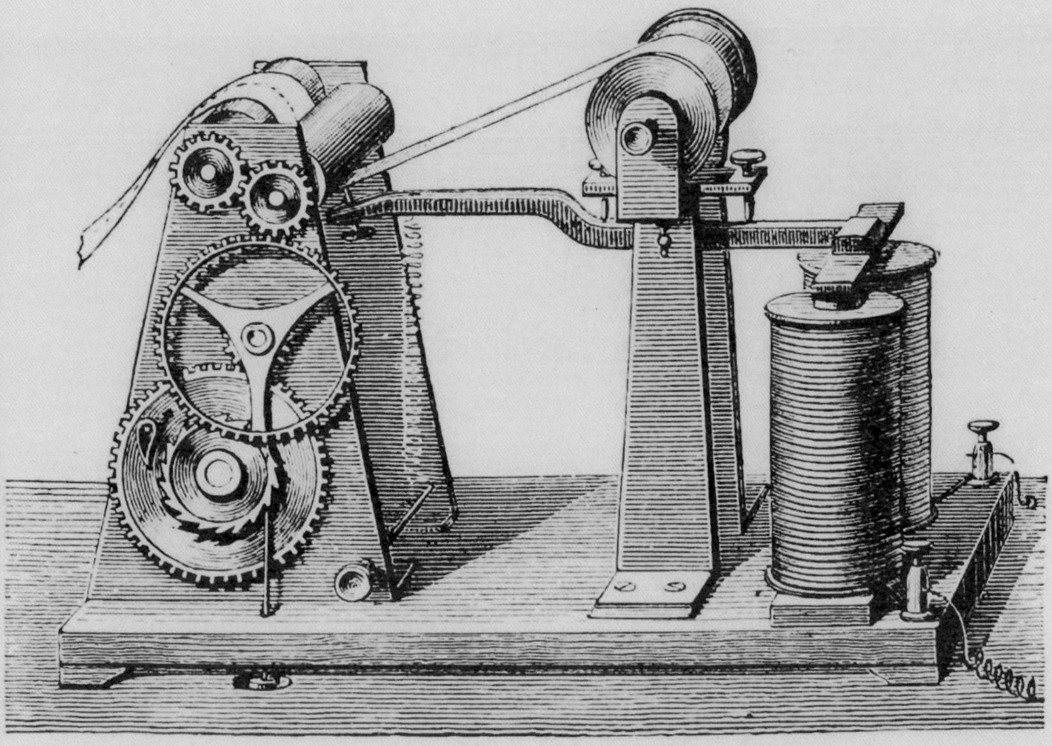

Vintage telegraph machine used to transmit Morse code (1873).

Comma	– – • • – –	2	• • – – –	6	– • • • •
Query	• • – – • •	3	• • • – –	7	– – • • •
0	– – – – –	4	• • • • –	8	– – – • •
1	• – – – –	5	• • • • •	9	– – – – •

"Look deep into nature, and then you will understand everything better."

Albert Einstein

LEVEL 2 »

WILDERNESS SURVIVAL

WILDERNESS SURVIVAL

Take it up a notch with real outdoor survival techniques. From building shelters to catching fish with a homemade trap, you'll discover how to thrive in the wild.

Whether you're hiking in the woods or dreaming of a jungle adventure, these tips will get you ready for the real deal!

"I think true wilderness can still be found, but it's hard to reach and dangerous when you get there, which is probably why it still exists."

Michelle Paver

HOW TO PURIFY WATER

Clean water is one of the most important things you need to survive. If you find water in the wild, you must make sure it's safe to drink, because it might have germs or dirt that can make you sick. Here's how to purify water in a survival situation.

STEP 1: FIND WATER

Look for water in streams, rivers, lakes, or rain puddles. Water runs downhill and so is most abundant in valleys and at the bottom of hills and mountains.

Avoid polluted water. You will notice it's polluted if it smells bad or is very cloudy.

EXPERT SURVIVAL TIP

Never drink untreated water. Even if it looks clear, it might still have harmful germs.

STEP 2: FILTER THE WATER

Before purifying, **remove dirt, leaves, or small bugs** from the water.

Use a cloth or bandana. Pour the water through the cloth to catch the big particles.

Make a simple filter. Use a bottle or container filled with layers of sand, gravel, and charcoal. Pour the water through the filter to make it clearer.

Simple filter set-up

Even water that looks clear and clean still requires filtering and purifying.

STEP 3: PURIFY THE WATER

This is the most important step to kill any germs.

Boiling

- Heat the water over a fire until it boils (big bubbles!).

- Let it boil for at least 1 minute to kill harmful germs.

Using purification tablets

- Drop a water purification tablet into your container of water and wait for the amount of time it says on the instructions (usually 30 minutes).

EXPERT SURVIVAL TIP

Practice at home. Try filtering and boiling water with an adult so you'll know what to do if you ever need to do it in the wild.

STEP 4: LET IT COOL AND DRINK

Once the water is clean and safe, let it cool if you boiled it. Then, drink up and stay hydrated!

COLLECTING WATER

Rain

Use anything you can find to collect water. You should be able to drink rainwater without purifying it, but following the previous steps will make the water even safer.

Dew

Leave a shirt or a sponge out overnight to collect the morning dew. Make sure to collect the items before the sun comes up and the water evaporates. Wring out the water into a container and then purify. Hey presto—drinking water!

WHERE TO SHELTER IN A SURVIVAL SITUATION

In a survival situation, finding or building a shelter is one of the most important things you can do. A good shelter keeps you warm, dry, and protected from weather, animals, and bugs.

LOCATION 101

Stay dry. Choose high ground or an area away from rivers, lakes, or places that might flood.

Avoid danger. Look out for falling rocks, dead tree branches, or animal tracks—they can mean danger.

Get close to resources. Try to be near clean water, firewood, and open space for signaling rescuers.

Consider wind and weather. Face your shelter entrance away from the wind to stay warm and dry.

EXPERT SURVIVAL TIP

Find the right spot for a shelter. A good shelter is all about location, as you have to consider safety, warmth, keeping dry, and using what's around you.

USE WHAT NATURE PROVIDES

Natural shelters. Look for caves, overhanging rocks, or large fallen trees that already provide cover. Make sure they're safe and free of hazards.

Thick trees or bushes. Dense trees can give you quick protection from rain or sun. Add branches and leaves to make it cozier.

BUILD YOUR OWN SHELTER

If you can't find natural shelter, here are some simple shelters you can build.

LEAN-TO SHELTER 101

• Find a sturdy stick or branch to use as the roof beam.

• Pile leaves, grass, and other soft materials on top to keep warm.

EXPERT SURVIVAL TIP

Stay warm. Pile leaves or grass where you'll sleep to keep you off the cold ground.

KENNEL 101

- Build an A-frame like a small tent out of sticks.
- Lean smaller branches against it at an angle, then cover with leaves, grass, or pine needles to block wind and rain.
- Add some branches on top to hold everything in place.

Always build shelters away from water sources like streams, lakes, and rivers. They might flood your shelter!

EXPERT SURVIVAL TIP

Block the wind. Use extra branches, rocks, or anything solid to close gaps in your shelter.

MAKING A CAMPFIRE

A campfire can keep you warm, cook your food, and even boost your spirits in a survival situation. But fire can also be dangerous if not handled carefully. With wildfires causing major damage in recent years, it's more important than ever to build fires responsibly.

CHOOSE A SAFE LOCATION

Find a clear area. Choose a spot at least 10 feet away from trees, bushes, or anything that could catch fire.

Dig a pit. Dig a small pit and surround it with rocks to contain the fire.

Clear the ground. Remove any dry leaves, grass, or sticks from around your fire area to prevent it from catching light.

BUILD THE FIRE PROPERLY

Gather materials. You'll need three types of wood:

- **Tinder** (small, dry stuff like leaves or paper)
- **Kindling** (small sticks about the size of your finger)
- **Fuel wood** (larger logs for a steady burn)

MAKE A FIRE STRUCTURE

Use the tipi method. Place tinder in the middle, then lean kindling around it in a cone shape. Add larger logs on the outside once it's burning well.

Light the fire. Use matches, a lighter, or a fire starter. Start with the tinder and gradually add kindling and fuel wood.

KEEP IT UNDER CONTROL

Stay nearby. Never leave your fire unattended. Even a small gust of wind can spread embers that could cause a wildfire.

Keep water or sand nearby. Always have a bucket of water or a pile of dirt nearby to quickly put out the fire if it gets out of control.

EXTINGUISH THE FIRE SAFELY

Spread the coals. Use a stick or shovel to spread the embers out.

Pour on water or dirt. Slowly pour water over the embers or cover them with dirt until all the hissing stops. Stir the ashes to make sure everything is wet or buried.

Double check. Feel the ashes with the back of your hand (carefully!). If they're still warm, the fire isn't completely out. Repeat the process.

WILDFIRE WARNINGS: WHY THIS MATTERS...

In recent years, wildfires have destroyed homes, forests, and wildlife habitats. Many of these fires were caused by unattended or poorly managed campfires.

Wildfires in the U.S. and Canada. 2023 saw a record-breaking number of wildfires, burning millions of acres and forcing thousands of people to evacuate.

Dry conditions. In hot, dry weather, even a single spark can ignite a massive fire.

By following these steps, you're helping protect not just yourself but also the environment and everyone around you.

WILDFIRE RISK

In areas with wildfire risk, campfires may be banned. Always check local rules before lighting a fire. If fires aren't allowed, stay warm by wearing layers or using a heat-reflective blanket.

Remember, fire is a powerful tool, but with great power comes great responsibility. Build it wisely, enjoy it safely, and always leave your campsite as you found it—or better!

MAKING SURVIVAL ROPE

From tying your shoes to making a climbing rope, nature provides all the raw materials you need. Nettle cord is one of the strongest natural cords and is easy to make with survival expert know-how!

STEP 1

1.

Collect the longest nettles you can find. Wear gloves to ensure you don't get stung. Cut the nettle at its base—DO NOT pull it up with its roots (it will grow again next year if you cut it).

2.

STEP 2

Strip all the leaves off the stem by running your hand from the base toward the top. Don't do it the other way around, as you may remove the material that you need to make the cord.

STEP 3

Lay the stem on a hard surface and gently pound it with a smooth stone. Use your thumbnail to open up the stem and lay it flat.

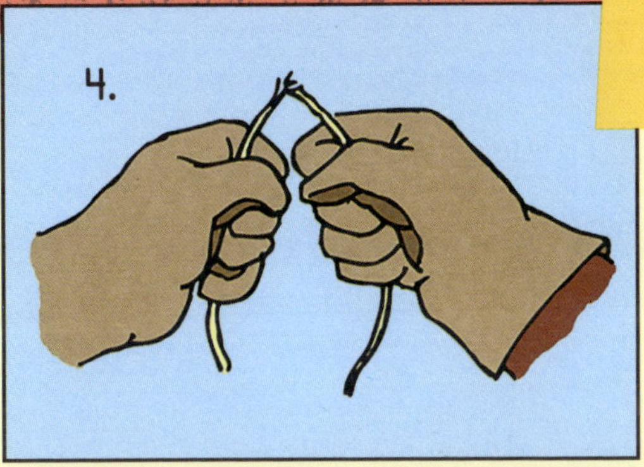

STEP 4

Estimate a point one-third up the stem and carefully fold the stem so the core breaks. You can now strip the outer material away from the core. Discard the inner core and hang the outer material to dry. It will soon be ready to be spun into cord.

Rope and cord can be made from a huge variety of things including thistles, vines, rushes, long grass, tree bark, and coconut husks.

STEP 5

Once the fibers are dry, they are ready to be spun into cord. Pick up one of the strands. Hold it in your hand so that two-thirds hangs to the right **(A)**, and one-third to the left **(B)**.

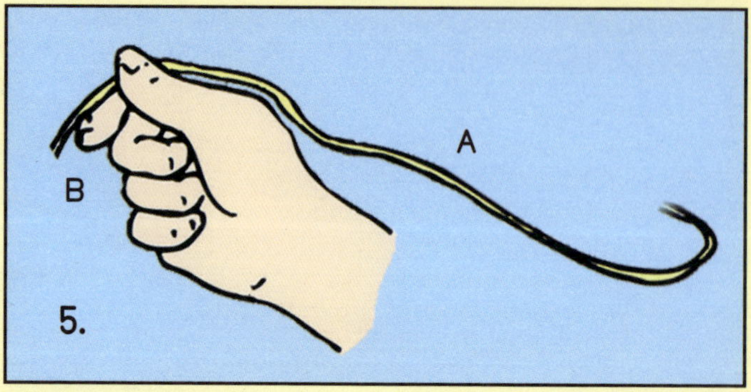

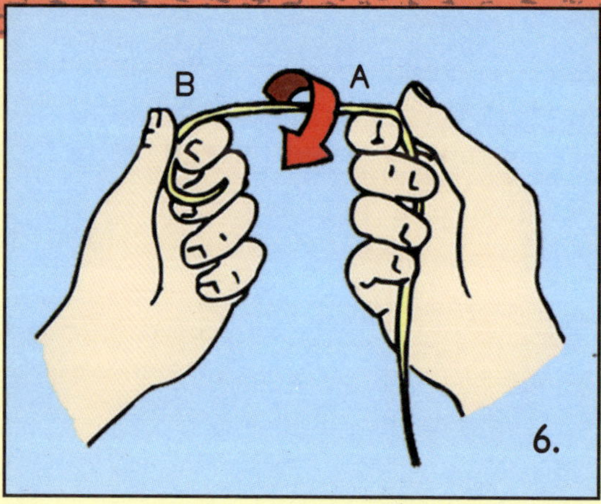

STEP 6

Holding **B** in your left hand, dampen the index finger and thumb of your right hand and roll the fiber between your fingers in a clockwise direction. Moving from left to right, twist the whole fiber into a strand.

STEP 7

To secure the twist, take the middle in your teeth and bring the two ends together. When you let go of the strand it will twist around itself. Repeat steps 1 to 6 with another fiber. Then take the two twisted strands **(A and B)** and wrap them around one another, as shown.

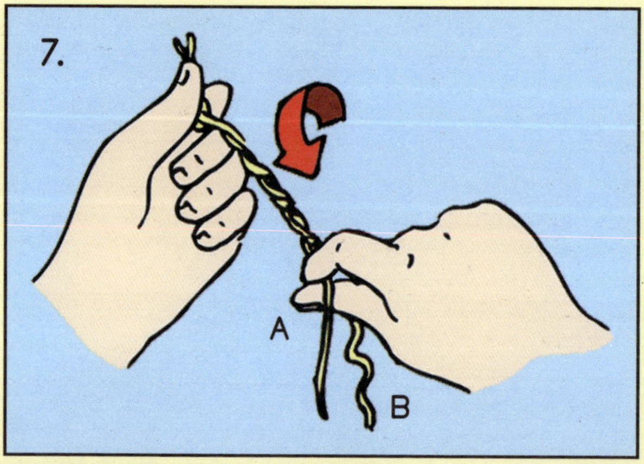

STEP 8

When knotted on the end, to keep it from unreeling, the result will be strong cordage that you can use for all your survival needs!

The Aztecs used to make bridges out of grass rope made using a similar technique.

SURVIVAL KNOTS 101

Learning to tie a few knots with your handmade cord will make your time in the wilderness even more fun! There are hundreds of knots for you to discover, but look up how to tie these particularly useful knots before your next adventure.

CLOVE HITCH

This is one of the most-tied knots. It can be used for tying things to a post or bar.

REEF KNOT

One of the first knots that you must learn to tie. Useful for tying something securely but also easy to undo. Don't tie it with a nylon cord or to a different-sized rope as it will come undone.

BOWLINE

This is a very easily tied loop that has many uses. It will not tighten or come undone when loaded with weight and so can be used as a lifeline.

TIMBER HITCH

Very secure and easy to undo. It can be used for dragging or securing things.

WILD PLANTS—SURVIVAL MEDICINE

Nature is full of helpful plants that can provide food, medicine, or tools in a survival situation. But always remember: not all plants are safe! Learn to identify the ones that are useful and never eat or use a plant unless you are with an outdoor instructor or survival expert who can assure you that it is 100% safe.

DANDELION

Where to find it:
Open fields, lawns, and roadsides.

Uses

Food: The entire plant is edible! The leaves can be eaten raw (like salad) or cooked for a less bitter taste. The roots can be boiled to make a tea.

Energy boost: The flowers and roots are rich in nutrients like vitamins A and C.

CATTAIL

Where to find it: Marshes, ponds, or along the edges of lakes and rivers.

Uses

Food: The roots and shoots are edible and taste like mild vegetables when cooked. The fluffy part at the top can be used as fire tinder.

Shelter: The long leaves can be woven together to make mats or roof coverings.

PLANTAIN (NOT THE BANANA!)

Where to find it: Fields, yards, and roadsides. Look for broad, green leaves that grow close to the ground.

Uses

First aid: Crush the leaves and place them on cuts, bug bites, or stings to help reduce pain and swelling.

Food: Young leaves can be eaten raw or cooked as a green vegetable.

PINE TREE

Where to find it:
Forests and wooded areas.

Uses
Food: Pine needles can be boiled to make a vitamin C-rich tea that keeps you hydrated and boosts your immune system.

Firestarter: Dry pine needles and resin are great for starting fires.

Emergency shelter: Use pine branches to build a lean-to or cover the ground to keep warm.

ALOE VERA (IN HOT CLIMATES)

Where to find it: Desert areas or warm, dry climates.

Uses
First aid: Break open the leaf and use the gel inside to soothe burns, sunburn, or insect bites.

CLOVER

Where to find it:
Fields, meadows, and lawns.

Uses
Food: Clover leaves and flowers are edible and can be added to soups or teas.

Nutrition: They provide vitamins and protein to keep your energy up.

WILD GARLIC OR ONION

Where to find it: Damp woods, meadows, or near streams. It smells like garlic or onion when crushed.

Uses
Food: Adds flavor to meals or can be eaten raw for energy.

Warning: Be careful not to confuse these with poisonous lookalikes like death camas. If it doesn't smell like onion or garlic, don't eat it!

SAFETY TIPS FOR WILD PLANTS

Learn to identify safely. Practice with an adult to identify plants correctly. Use guidebooks or apps to help.
Don't eat unknown plants. If you're not 100% sure it's safe, don't touch or eat it—some plants are poisonous.
Test carefully. If you must eat an unknown plant, follow the "Universal Edibility Test" with an adult's help to avoid getting sick.

THE UNIVERSAL EDIBILITY TEST

If you're lost in the wild and unsure if a plant is safe to eat, the Universal Edibility Test can help you to find out. It's a step-by-step process to test if a plant is safe—but use it only as a last resort! Eating the wrong plant can make you very sick and you should never eat a wild plant unless it has been clearly identified as being edible and safe by an adult.

IMPORTANT WARNINGS BEFORE YOU START

Be patient. The whole test can take hours—don't rush it.

Test only one part of the plant. Leaves, berries, roots, and flowers can have different effects, so test each part separately.

Avoid dangerous plants. Don't test plants with the following features:

- A strong or bitter smell
- Milky or colored sap
- Spines, thorns, or fine hairs
- Three-leaf clusters (like poison ivy)

Step 1: Identify the plant

Look at the plant and try to identify it using a guidebook or app. Avoid anything you suspect might be poisonous.

Step 2: Separate the plant parts

Separate the leaves, berries, flowers, and roots. Test only one part at a time.

EXPERT SURVIVAL TIP

This test is only for emergency survival use! You should always identify plants in order to determine if they are safe to eat!

Step 3: Do a skin test

Rub a small piece of the plant on your skin (like your wrist or inner elbow).

Wait for **15 minutes.** If your skin gets red, itchy, or irritated, don't eat the plant!

Step 4: Do a lip test

Place a tiny piece of the plant on your lips. Wait for **15 minutes.**

If your lips tingle, burn, or feel weird, don't eat it!

Step 5: Taste without swallowing

Put a small piece in your mouth and chew it. Don't swallow yet! Wait for **15 minutes.**

If you feel numbness, burning, or sickness, spit it out immediately.

Step 6: Swallow a small bite

If there are no bad effects, swallow a small piece. Wait for **4–6 hours** to see if you feel sick.

If you feel fine, it's probably safe to eat.

KEEP IN MIND

Test each plant part. Just because the leaves are safe doesn't mean the berries are. Repeat the test for each part of the plant.

Eat small amounts. Even if the plant seems safe, start by eating it in small amounts.

WHEN TO AVOID TESTING

If you have other food options or can survive without eating the plant, it's safer to leave it alone. This test is for emergencies only!

SURVIVAL FACT

The Universal Edibility Test was developed by U.S. Army survival experts.

SURVIVING A RIP CURRENT

Rip currents are strong, narrow currents that pull water—and anything in it—away from the shore. You can't always see a rip current, so it's important to know what to do if you find yourself being pulled away from the shore.

STAY CALM

Don't panic! Rip currents don't pull you under the water, but they can pull you away from shore.

Tread water and take deep breaths. This will help you to conserve energy and stay calm.

DON'T FIGHT THE CURRENT

Don't try to swim straight back to shore. Fighting the current will exhaust you—even the strongest swimmers can't outswim a rip current.

SWIM PARALLEL TO SHORE

Swim sideways, parallel to the shore, to escape the rip current. Rip currents are usually narrow (30-100 feet wide), so you can swim out of them.

Once you're out of the current, **turn and swim back to the shore at an angle** to avoid reentering the rip current.

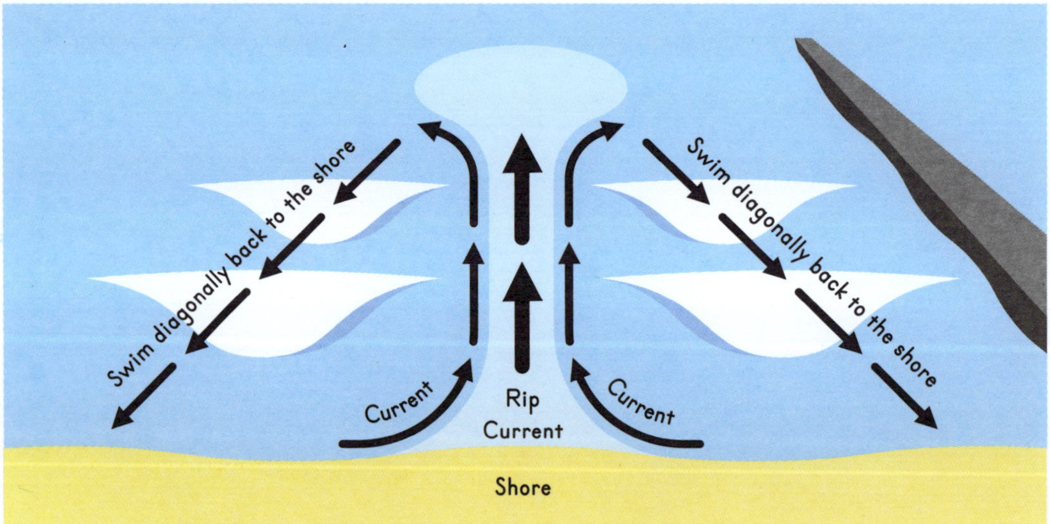

EXPERT SURVIVAL TIP

Rip currents are powerful, but not unbeatable. Staying calm, treading water, and knowing how to escape by swimming parallel to the shore are your best defenses.

FLOAT AND SIGNAL FOR HELP IF YOU'RE TIRED

If you can't swim out of a current, **float on your back** to conserve energy and let the current carry you.

Wave your arms and shout for help so the lifeguards can spot you.

HOW TO AVOID RIP CURRENTS

Check the water before swimming. Look for signs of rip currents, like water moving quickly away from shore, a gap in the waves, or foamy, choppy water.

Swim at lifeguarded beaches. Lifeguards are trained to spot and rescue swimmers from rip currents. Always be aware of where they are.

Pay attention to warning flags. A red flag means dangerous conditions, including rip currents.

HOW TO ESCAPE FROM QUICKSAND

Quicksand sounds like a nightmare survival situation, but with the right steps, you can escape! The key is to stay calm and move slowly—panicking will only make things worse!

STAY CALM

Don't panic! Quicksand won't pull you under like in the movies, but struggling can make you sink deeper.

LIGHTEN YOUR LOAD

Carefully remove any heavy bags or gear to make yourself lighter. Throw it to solid ground if possible.

SPREAD YOUR WEIGHT

Lean back and try to lie on your back. Spreading out your body increases your surface area and keeps you from sinking further.

EXPERT SURVIVAL TIP

Quicksand is much denser than you are. If you lie flat, you shouldn't sink below waist deep.

WIGGLE SLOWLY

Move backward in slow motion, wiggling your legs and making large sweeping arcs with your arms. Try to keep your breathing calm.

CRAWL TO SAFETY

Once you're free, **do not immediately stand up.** Crawl or roll to solid ground to spread your weight and avoid sinking again.

USE SOMETHING TO PULL YOURSELF OUT

If there is one available, **grab a stick, branch, or solid object nearby** to pull yourself out.

If someone is with you, get them to gently pull you out, while they stand at a safe distance on solid ground.

Look for danger zones! Quicksand is often found near riverbanks, marshes, or beaches. Use a stick to check the firmness of the ground ahead of you when hiking through this type of terrain.

ANIMAL TRACKING

Being able to identify animal tracks is like reading a story written on the ground—and in a survival situation, it could save your life!

TRACKING 101

Here's why it's so important...

Know what animals are nearby. By recognizing tracks, you can tell if potentially dangerous animals like bears, wolves, or mountain lions are in the area, giving you time to stay alert or change your path.

Find safe water and food sources. Tracks near streams or ponds can lead you to water or show you where animals gather, which might help you locate edible plants or small game.

Avoid surprise encounters. Spotting fresh tracks can warn you if an animal is close, helping you avoid a dangerous encounter.

HOW TO IDENTIFY TRACKS

Look at the size and shape. Is a print large with claw marks, like a bear's, or smaller and round, like a deer's?

Count the toes. Many animals leave distinct patterns with specific numbers of toes, such as four for dogs and cats, or two for deer (their two middle toes support most of their weight).

Notice the depth and spacing. Deep prints may mean a heavy animal, while closely spaced prints could mean the animal is moving slowly.

Can you guess which animal this print belongs to?

Answer: dog

PRACTICE MAKES PERFECT

Take time to learn the tracks of animals in your area before you venture into the wild. Knowing what to look for can make you more aware of your surroundings and help you to stay one step ahead!

Here are some common tracks for you to look out for when you're next in the wilderness...

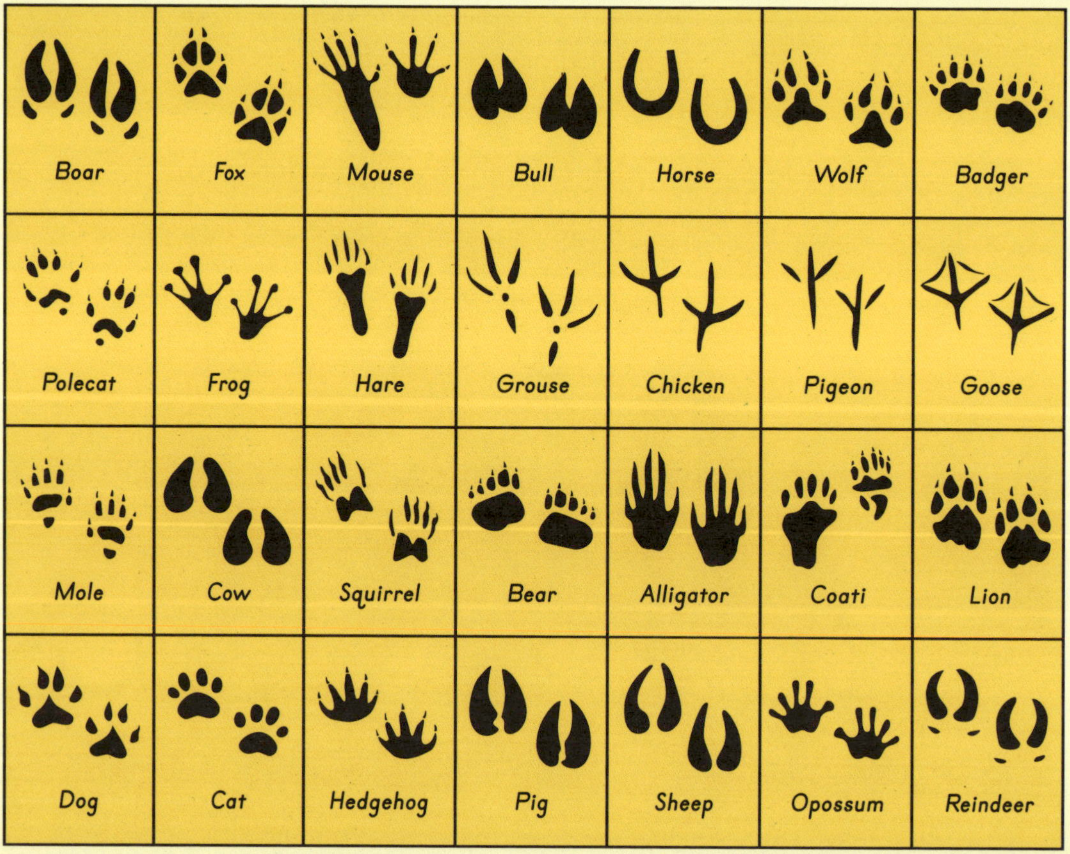

MAKING YOUR OWN TRACK CASTS

Making casts of animal tracks is a fun and exciting way to connect with nature while learning more about the wildlife around you! By creating a plaster cast of an individual print, you can preserve the moment that you discovered it forever—a perfect memento for your outdoor survival adventures! So, grab some plaster and start capturing the stories written in the ground—you never know what amazing creatures you might discover!

You will need:

- Plaster of Paris
- 2 cups of water
- A jug • A bowl • A spoon

1. First, mix together the plaster of Paris with water (approx 1 cup of powder to 2 cups of water).

EXPERT TIP

Paint your cast with dark paint to make the distinctive features stand out. You could make an entire rainbow of animal track casts!

2. Pour the plaster into the print.

3. Leave to dry. Do not touch for at least five hours, even if it looks dry. When the plaster is dry, remove it from the print.

“Going to the woods is going home, for I suppose we came from the woods originally. But in some of nature’s forests, the adventurous traveler seems a feeble, unwelcome creature; wild beasts and the weather trying to kill him, the rank, tangled vegetation, armed with spears and stinging needles, barring his way and making life a hard struggle.”

JOHN MUIR

WILDERNESS FISHING

If you're stuck in the wilderness, fishing with a bottle trap is a low-effort, high-reward way to secure food—and it's pretty exciting to see what you catch! Let's dive in.

HOW TO MAKE A BOTTLE TRAP 101

You will need:

- Empty plastic bottle
- Sharp knife
- Yarn or tape
- Bait (worms, bugs, or anything smelly)

WARNING!

Please ask an adult adventurer to help you cut the top off the bottle. Do not use sharp knives unsupervised.

EXPERT SURVIVAL TIPS

Location, location, location! Place the trap where fish naturally gather, like near reeds or overhanging branches.

Use the right bait. If you're unsure, try experimenting—fish love anything smelly and edible!

1. Find a plastic bottle. Look for any large bottle, like a soda or water bottle. Bigger is better, as it can catch larger fish.

2. Cut off the top of the bottle. Use a knife or sharp rock to carefully cut off the top of the bottle, about a quarter to a third of the way down.

3. Flip the top. Turn the top part upside down (so it looks like a funnel) and fit it back into the bottle's bottom half. Secure it with yarn or tape if you have some.

4. Add bait. Fish can't resist a good snack! Add small insects, worms, or bits of food to the bottle to lure them in.

5. Place it in the water. Submerge the bottle in a stream, pond, or lake where fish swim. Use rocks to weigh it down, but make sure the open end is easy for fish to enter.

6. Check your trap. Leave it for a few hours and come back to see if you've got any visitors. The fish will swim in through the funnel but won't figure out how to get out.

AFTER THE CATCH

Prepare your meal. Cook your catch (under adult supervision) over an open fire, making sure the fish is cooked through.

EXPERT SURVIVAL TIPS

Stay patient. Fishing with a trap takes time, so use the waiting period to work on other survival tasks, like building a fire or shelter.

Best fishing times. Just before dawn or just after dusk are the best times to fish. A full moon and an approaching storm can also make fish more active.

EXPERT SURVIVAL TIP

Do not cook fish on an open fire in bear territory. The smell will attract them from miles around!

"Survival can be summed up in three words—never give up. That's the heart of it, really. Just keep trying."

Bear Grylls

LEVEL 3 »

EXTREME SURVIVAL

EXTREME SURVIVAL

What happens when nature gets intense? In this level, you'll learn how to stay safe during natural disasters like earthquakes or tsunamis. You'll also discover how to handle dangerous animal encounters, like facing off with a bear or a shark.

It's extreme, it's exciting, and it's all about staying calm under pressure.

“There are very few wild animals that can’t run down a human being; the big predators would run down Usain Bolt without even thinking about it. So your only chance is to stand your ground!”

STEVE BACKSHALL

There are populations of grizzly bears in Western Canada, Alaska, Idaho, Montana, Washington, and Wyoming. They were formerly hunted to near extinction.

BEAR ATTACK!

Although most bears will stay away from humans, if you ever find yourself face-to-face with a grizzly bear, don't panic! Here's what you need to do to survive...

GRIZZLY BEARS 101

Standing height: 8 ft

Max weight: 800 pounds

1. Stay calm and don't run. Running can make the bear think you're prey, and it might chase you. Don't climb a tree either—bears are excellent climbers!

2. Make yourself look big. Stand tall, wave your arms, and talk to the bear in a calm voice to show that you're not scared and you're not a threat.

3. Back away slowly. If the bear isn't coming toward you, start walking backward slowly. Never turn your back to the bear.

4. Play dead if it charges. If the bear comes at you, lie on the ground, curl up into a ball, cover your neck with your hands, and stay still. The bear will likely lose interest if it thinks you're not a threat.

5. Wait for the bear to leave. Keep calm and stay in your ball position until the bear is far away.

Remember, grizzly bears usually don't want to hurt you—staying calm and smart can keep you safe!

EXPERT SURVIVAL TIP

Travel in a group while in bear territory. Bears will shy away from the smell of groups of people.

NOT ALL BEARS ARE THE SAME!

Read on to learn the bear necessities for surviving attacks by other types of bear.

AMERICAN BLACK BEARS 101

Standing height: 5-7 ft
Max weight: 500 pounds

Use the same survival tactics as for the grizzly bear, but...

Do NOT play dead. This is a key difference! If a black bear charges or attacks, **fight back**! Use sticks, rocks, or anything nearby to protect yourself and make lots of noise. Black bears can be scared off if they see you're not an easy target.

EXPERT SURVIVAL TIP

Make lots of noise if you think a bear is watching you. This can scare it away before you even see it!

POLAR BEARS 101

Standing height: 10 ft
Max weight: 1,700 pounds

If you ever find yourself near a **polar bear**, it's important to know that polar bears are the **most dangerous of all bears**. The best survival tactic for confrontations with this bear is to make sure that you do not risk being in a face-to-face position in their territory!

Do NOT heat food outside. Polar bears have an excellent sense of smell, and you will attract hungry polar bears from miles around!

Do NOT camp in polar bear territory. A tent provides no protection from a polar bear attack. Always stay in a building with a solid wood or masonry construction.

Do NOT play dead. This is really important! If a polar bear attacks, playing dead will not work. You must fight back with anything you can. Use sticks and rocks, and if that doesn't work—run!

EXPERT SURVIVAL TIP

Always carry bear pepper spray when traveling through areas with a bear population. Bear spray will stop most bears in their tracks and provide you with enough time to get away safely.

SHARK ATTACK!

If you ever find yourself face-to-fin with a shark in the water, don't panic! Here's how to stay safe...

Tiger shark.

SHARK 101

1. Stay calm and don't splash around! Splashing can make the shark think you're prey, so stay as still as possible.

2. Face the shark. Sharks like to surprise their prey, so if you can face it, it's less likely to attack.

3. Slowly back away toward the shore or boat. Move smoothly and steadily, keeping your movements calm to avoid attracting the shark's attention.

4. Defend yourself if the shark gets close. If it tries to bite, aim for sensitive spots like the **eyes, gills,** or **nose.** Punch, kick, or use anything you have to protect yourself, like a snorkel or camera.

5. Get out of the water as fast as possible. Once you're safe, report the sighting to help others stay aware.

Remember—sharks are curious but rarely attack humans. Staying calm and prepared can make all the difference!

Great white shark (left and right).

EXPERT SURVIVAL TIP

Don't wear jewelry in the ocean. Sharks can mistake glinting jewelry for fish scales.

The Florida Museum of Natural History's International Shark Attack File is one of the foremost authorities on shark attacks in the world.

In 2023, the International Shark Attack File investigated 120 alleged shark-human interactions worldwide. It confirmed 69 unprovoked shark bites on humans and 22 provoked bites.

USA topped the charts with 36 attacks, two of which were fatal.

Australia was second with 15 attacks, four of which were fatal.

TOP TIPS FOR AVOIDING A SHARK ENCOUNTER

Swim in groups. Sharks are less likely to approach if you're with other people.

Avoid swimming at dawn, dusk, or night. These are the times that sharks are most active when hunting.

Stay out of the water if you're bleeding. Sharks can detect even small amounts of blood from far away.

Avoid areas with large numbers of prey animals. Keep out of the water in areas where there are large numbers of seals or large schools of fish.

Avoid swimming near ledges. Sharks love areas where the ocean floor suddenly drops away, as it makes ambush attacks easier. Avoid beaches with steep seafloor shelves.

Bull shark.

DANGEROUS SPECIES

There are hundreds of shark species, but only three are responsible for most fatal unprovoked attacks on humans: they are the great white, tiger, and bull shark.

BULL SHARK ☠☠

Max length: 13 ft
Max weight: 700 lb

Bull sharks use a "bump-and-bite" method to catch prey—they bump and bite their prey until it is too tired to swim away.

TIGER SHARK ☠

Max length: 18 ft
Max weight: 2,000 lb

Tiger sharks are very aggressive and will prey on anything that is near the ocean's surface.

GREAT WHITE ☠☠☠

Max length: 20 ft
Max weight: 4,500 lb

Great white sharks ambush their prey in surprise attacks, swimming up from below at speed, then biting with their powerful jaws.

MOUNTAIN LION ATTACK!

Mountain lions inhabit a wide range of habitats from forests and mountains to deserts and wetlands. They live across the wildernesses of America and sometimes attack humans. Here are some top survival tips if you encounter one of these majestic beasts out on the trails.

MOUNTAIN LION 101

Length: 8 ft
Max weight: 150 lbs

1. Stay calm and don't run. Running can trigger the mountain lion's instinct to chase. Stand your ground.

2. Make yourself look big and intimidating. Stand tall, wave your arms slowly, open your jacket, and speak firmly in a loud voice. Let the mountain lion know you're not prey.

3. Maintain eye contact and never turn your back. Slowly back away while facing the mountain lion. Don't crouch down or bend over, as this can make you look like an easy target.

4. Throw objects if it gets too close. Toss rocks, sticks, or anything you can grab to scare it off. Aim near the animal, not directly at it—unless it's attacking.

5. Fight back if attacked. Use sticks, rocks, or even your fists to defend yourself, focusing on sensitive areas like the eyes and nose. Show the mountain lion that you won't go down easily.

EXPERT SURVIVAL TIPS TO AVOID AN ENCOUNTER

- **Don't hike alone.** Travel in groups and keep children close.
- **Avoid dawn and dusk outings.** These are prime hunting times for mountain lions.
- **Keep pets on a leash.** Pets can attract mountain lions, so don't let them wander.
- **Make noise as you hike.** Talking, clapping, or using a bell can alert animals to your presence and prevent surprises.

By staying calm, looking big, and fighting back, if necessary, you can keep yourself safe in mountain lion territory!

The mountain lion is also referred to as a cougar, panther, catamount, and puma. It is the most widespread wild land mammal in the Western Hemisphere.

SNAKE ATTACK!

Most snakes are not aggressive and prefer to avoid humans. However, North America is home to many snake species, including venomous ones like rattlesnakes, cottonmouths, copperheads, and coral snakes. Here's how to stay safe, avoid bites, and what to do if you are bitten.

AVOIDING A SNAKE ATTACK

Watch your step. Stick to clear paths and avoid walking through thick brush. Snakes like to hide in tall grass, rocks, and logs. Always look where you're walking or placing your hands.

Use a stick to probe ahead. This can be useful if you're moving through brush, tall grass, or a forest. A stick can help to flush out snakes that are hiding in the undergrowth.

Never reach into dark holes or under logs. This is where snakes tend to lurk, so always be vigilant and use common sense.

Stay calm if you see a snake. Don't approach it or provoke it. Most snakes bite when they feel threatened. Slowly back away and give the snake plenty of space.

Wear protective gear. Thick boots and long pants can reduce the risk of a bite.

IDENTIFYING NORTH AMERICA'S VENOMOUS SNAKES

There are 30 species of venomous snake in North America, but most are species of the below types of snake. Around 8,000 people are bitten each year.

RATTLESNAKES

Max length: 8 ft.
Max weight: 10 lbs

Found in deserts, forests, and grasslands. Recognizable by their rattling tails and triangular heads.

The eastern diamondback rattlesnake is the largest venomous snake in North America.

COPPERHEADS

Max length: 3 ft
Max weight: 12⅛ oz

Found in wooded areas, especially in the eastern US. They have coppery-brown, hourglass-shaped patterns.

COTTONMOUTHS (WATER MOCCASINS)

Max length: 6 ft
Max weight: 4.4 lbs

Found near swamps, rivers, and lakes in the Southeast. Known for their open, white mouths when threatened.

Copperheads spend a lot of time in the water and rarely bite humans. However, their venom can be deadly if an antivenom isn't administered.

CORAL SNAKES

Max length: 3 ft
Max weight: 11 oz

A small snake found in the southeast with distinctive bright red, yellow, and black bands. They have an incredibly potent venom, but bites are very rare.

WHAT TO DO IF YOU'RE BITTEN BY A SNAKE

If you are unfortunate enough to be bitten by a snake, these steps will help you think calmly when under pressure and survive an attack.

STAY CALM AND STILL

Try not to panic. Panic increases your heart rate, spreading venom faster. Try to stay as still as possible.

IDENTIFY THE SNAKE

Take note of the snake's appearance if it is safe to do so. This will help medical professionals. Don't risk being bitten again.

CALL FOR HELP

Dial 911 or have someone take you to the nearest ER.

IF YOU CAN'T GET MEDICAL HELP IMMEDIATELY

Keep the bite area still. Immobilize the area and keep it below heart level to slow venom spread.

Wash the bite. Rinse the area with clean water to remove dirt.

Remove tight items. Take off rings, watches, or anything that could restrict blood flow as swelling occurs.

Hydrate. Drink water to stay hydrated.

Seek shelter. Protect yourself from the elements while waiting for rescue.

DO NOT

Try to suck out the venom. This simply doesn't work!

Apply ice or a tourniquet. These can make the bite effects worse.

CROCODILE, CAIMAN, OR ALLIGATOR ATTACK!

Crocodiles, caimans, and alligators are powerful predators, known for their strength and speed in the water. While attacks on humans are rare, they can occur, especially if these reptiles feel threatened. Understanding how to survive these encounters is crucial if you are exploring areas these creatures are known to inhabit.

AMERICAN CROCODILE

Max length: 20 ft
Max weight: 1,900 lbs

CAIMAN

Max length: 8.2 ft
Max weight: 128 lbs

AMERICAN ALLIGATOR

Max length: 15 ft
Max weight: 1,000 lbs

BEFORE AN ENCOUNTER

Stay alert near water. Crocodiles, caimans, and alligators are often found in rivers, swamps, and lakes. Avoid swimming in areas where they are known to live. Always be vigilant, especially during the reptiles' feeding times and breeding season.

Keep your distance from the water's edge. These animals can lunge out of the water faster than you'd expect.

Know the signs. If you see warning signs for crocodiles or alligators in an area, respect them and stay away.

IF YOU ENCOUNTER A CROCODILE OR ALLIGATOR

Do not approach. Stay calm and back away slowly. Do not make sudden movements or loud noises that could provoke the animal.

Do not run in zigzags. Despite myths, running in a straight line is your best bet. These animals are fast in short bursts but tire quickly.

IF YOU'RE ATTACKED

Fight back. Aim for the eyes and snout. These are sensitive areas and can make the animal release you. Use any tools you have, like a stick, rock, or even your fists.

Resist the roll. Crocodiles and alligators use a deadly move called the "death roll," where they spin to tear apart prey. Fight to stay upright and resist being pulled underwater.

Get to safety. Once you have freed yourself, get as far away as possible. Even if the creature seems to have moved on, don't linger in the area—it could return and attack again. When you're safe, seek medical attention, as bites can lead to severe infections.

Stay away from water in areas that are known to have crocodile, caiman, or alligator populations.

IF YOU'RE IN WATER

Stay calm. Splashing and panicking will attract the animal. Stay still and try to back away quietly.

Find high ground. If possible, climb a tree or a rockface to get out of reach. Stay there until it's safe.

HOW TO AVOID FUTURE ATTACKS

Be cautious at night. Crocodiles and alligators are nocturnal hunters, meaning they are more active after dark.

Travel with a group. There's safety in numbers, and these animals are less likely to attack large groups.

Respect their habitat. These creatures are not normally aggressive—they just like to defend their territory. Stay out of their habitat to avoid trouble!

SURVIVING A TSUNAMI!

Surviving a tsunami starts with preparation and quick action. Tsunamis are powerful and fast, but by knowing what to do, you can keep yourself and your loved ones safe. Here's how to stay safe before, during, and after a tsunami...

BEFORE A TSUNAMI

Know the warning signs. A sudden withdrawal of water from the shore, a loud roaring sound from the ocean, or an earthquake can signal an approaching tsunami.

Have an evacuation plan. Know the safest, highest ground near your area and the fastest routes to get there. Share the plan with your family or group.

Stay informed. Sign up for emergency alerts and pay attention to warnings from local authorities.

Tsunamis travel over open oceans as fast as an airplane, reaching speeds of over 500 miles per hour!

DURING A TSUNAMI

Move to high ground immediately. If you see the water recede or feel a strong earthquake, don't wait for an official warning—head to the highest ground as quickly as possible.

Stay away from the shore. Never go down to the beach to watch the waves. Tsunamis move faster than you can run!

Climb or find shelter. If there is not enough time to evacuate, climb to the highest, safest place you can find, such as a sturdy building or tall tree.

EXPERT SURVIVAL TIPS

Pack an emergency kit. Include water, food, first-aid supplies, flashlights, and a whistle to signal for help.

Know the geography. Tsunamis are more likely in coastal earthquake-prone areas. Be aware of evacuation zones and safe locations near you.

Practice evacuation drills. Familiarize yourself with escape routes to react quickly in an emergency.

AFTER A TSUNAMI

Wait for the all-clear. Multiple waves can follow the first one, so never assume it's safe until authorities officially declare it.

Avoid flooded areas. The water may be contaminated with debris, chemicals, or sewage. Do not enter these areas, as they pose significant health risks.

Help others if it is safe. Assist people who may be injured or trapped, but prioritize your own safety. Do not put yourself at risk in the process.

Tsunamis are serious, but with preparation and swift action, you can survive and stay safe. Remember, high ground and fast thinking are your best defenses!

SURVIVING AN EARTHQUAKE!

Earthquakes can strike without warning, so knowing what to do when disaster strikes is vital. The key is to stay calm and protect yourself from falling objects and debris. If you live in an area where earthquakes occur, take time to swot up on these top survival tips.

BEFORE AN EARTHQUAKE

Plan ahead. Know all the safe spots in your home, like under sturdy tables or against interior walls.

Secure heavy objects. Talk to your parents about fastening heavy objects to the walls, like bookcases and TVs.

DURING AN EARTHQUAKE

If you're inside...

Drop, cover, and hold on!

- **Drop** to your hands and knees to avoid being knocked over.
- **Cover** your head and neck with your arms and get under a sturdy table.

- **Hold on** to furniture to stay protected from falling debris.

Stay away from windows. Glass can shatter, so move away from windows, mirrors, and other breakable items.

Do not run outside. Stay put until the shaking stops. Running outside can be dangerous due to falling debris, like bricks or glass.

EXPERT SURVIVAL TIP

If you notice a dog or a flock of birds behaving oddly, or lakes and ponds giving off an eggy smell, this could be a warning that an earthquake is imminent.

IF YOU'RE OUTSIDE

Move to an open area. Stay away from buildings, trees, power lines, and anything that could fall.

Drop and cover. Get low and protect your head until the shaking stops.

Earthquakes can be terrifying, but staying calm and knowing what to do can keep you safe. Protect yourself during the shaking and be extra cautious afterward.

IF YOU'RE IN A CAR

Pull over safely. Stop in an open area, away from bridges, overpasses, and trees.

Stay in the car. Keep your seatbelt on and wait for the shaking to stop.

EXPERT SURVIVAL TIPS

Keep an emergency kit. The best thing you can do is keep a kit ready with water, food, a flashlight, and a whistle.

Keep shoes nearby. Earthquakes can shatter glass and cause debris, so keep sturdy shoes by your bed.

Practice makes perfect. The more you practice earthquake drills, the calmer and safer you'll be in a real quake.

AFTER AN EARTHQUAKE

Check yourself for injuries. Treat minor wounds with a first-aid kit and call for help if someone is seriously hurt.

Avoid unsafe buildings. Aftershocks can cause damaged structures to collapse, so always make sure to stay outside if the building looks unsafe.

Be careful of hazards. Watch for broken glass, fallen power lines, and gas leaks (don't light matches or turn on electrical switches if you smell gas).

Listen for updates. Use a battery-powered radio or phone to get information about aftershocks and emergency instructions.

SURVIVING A TORNADO!

Tornadoes are powerful and dangerous storms that can cause significant damage in a short amount of time, but with the right plan, you can stay safe. The key is to act quickly and know where to go.

BEFORE A TORNADO

Know the warning signs

- Dark, greenish skies
- Large hail or a loud roaring sound like a freight train
- A funnel cloud or swirling debris

HAVE A PLAN

Know where the safest spot in your home is, like a storm cellar, basement, or an interior room with no windows.

Practice tornado drills with your family so everyone knows what to do.

BUILD AN EMERGENCY KIT

Include water, snacks, a flashlight, a whistle, a first-aid kit, and a battery-powered radio to get updates.

EXPERT SURVIVAL TIP

A **"Tornado Watch"** means conditions are right for tornadoes—be prepared.

A **"Tornado Warning"** means a tornado has been spotted—take shelter immediately!

DURING A TORNADO

If you're inside...

Go to a safe spot. Head to the basement, storm cellar, or an interior room on the lowest floor.

Stay away from windows. Windows will most likely smash during a tornado, spreading lots of glass.

PROTECT YOURSELF

Get under a sturdy piece of furniture like a table or desk.

Cover your head and neck with your arms, a blanket, or a mattress for extra protection.

IF YOU'RE OUTSIDE...

Get to shelter. If you can reach a sturdy building, go there immediately.

Avoid bridges or overpasses—they can be more dangerous during a tornado.

Lie flat in a low area. If there's no shelter, find a ditch or low spot, and lie flat on your stomach.

Cover your head and neck with your hands to protect yourself from flying debris.

IF YOU'RE IN A CAR...

Don't try to outrun the tornado. Tornadoes can change direction quickly and are faster than they look.

Abandon the car if necessary. If the tornado is close, get out of the car and lie flat in a ditch or low area, covering your head.

EXPERT SURVIVAL TIP

Don't wait! If you see a tornado, act fast. Seconds count!

AFTER A TORNADO

Stay safe. Watch out for broken glass, downed power lines, or sharp debris.

Avoid damaged buildings—they might collapse. Stay away from walls, ceilings, or broken windows.

Listen for updates. Use a radio or phone to get news about further storms or rescue efforts.

Help others. Check if people nearby need assistance, but make sure you're safe first.

SURVIVING A WILDFIRE IN THE WILDERNESS!

Wildfires are one of the most dangerous situations you can face in the wilderness. They move fast, change direction, and will burn everything in their path. But with quick thinking and the right actions, you can escape safely.

SPOT THE SIGNS OF A WILDFIRE

Smoke in the distance. A hazy sky or a strong smell of smoke can mean a wildfire is nearby.

Sudden changes in wind. Wildfires create their own weather patterns, causing gusts or shifts in wind direction.

Crackling sounds or glowing sky. Flames may be closer than they seem if you hear crackling or see a red glow, especially at night.

MOVE AWAY QUICKLY

Head toward safety. Move away from the fire and toward open areas with less vegetation, such as rocky outcrops, bodies of water, or cleared ground.

Travel downhill if the fire is on a slope. Fires move faster uphill due to rising heat.

Stay upwind. Move so the wind is blowing smoke and fire away from you—not toward you. Be aware of the wind's direction, as it can quickly change.

PROTECT YOUR BREATHING

Cover your nose and mouth. Use a damp cloth, bandana, or shirt to filter out smoke and make breathing easier.

Stay low. Smoke rises, so crouch or crawl close to the ground where the air is clearer. If you are near heavy smoke, crouch or crawl to stay as close to the ground as possible.

CROSS TO SAFETY IF POSSIBLE

Find natural barriers. Cross a stream, river, or lake to put a natural barrier between you and the fire. Avoid areas with thick vegetation or dry grass—they burn quickly!

IF YOU CAN'T ESCAPE THE FIRE

Find a safe zone. Look for a large, open area like a bare hillside, rockface, or water.

Dig a shallow trench or clear away vegetation to create a fire break.

Lie flat on the ground and cover yourself with dirt, rocks, or a fire-resistant blanket.

Stay low and breathe through a cloth to avoid inhaling too much smoke. Remain in place until the fire has passed.

SIGNAL FOR HELP

Use bright colors or reflective items.

Wave a brightly colored cloth or use a mirror to signal to rescuers.

Shout or whistle. Make noise to help others locate you if visibility is poor.

PREVENTING WILDFIRES

Be careful with fires. Never leave a campfire unattended and fully extinguish it before leaving.

Follow local rules. Many wilderness areas restrict fires during dry seasons. Respect these guidelines.

Know the conditions. Avoid hiking in areas with high fire danger, especially during windy, dry weather.

WARNING!

If you believe you've spotted a fire,

ALWAYS CALL 911.

This will notify and dispatch the appropriate emergency personnel to tackle the blaze.

> "The supernatural is the natural not yet understood."
>
> Elbert Hubbard

LEVEL 4 »

SUPERNATURAL SURVIVAL

SUPERNATURAL SURVIVAL

Dare to enter the spooky side of survival? From escaping a haunted house to surviving werewolves, vampires, and even alien invasions, this level is for adventurers with big imaginations!

You'll have loads of fun learning how to outsmart things that go bump in the night (even if they only exist in stories).

> “I love the idea that magic and witchcraft and battles between supernatural creatures could be raging all around us, but just out of sight.”

Anthony Horowitz

SURVIVING A VAMPIRE ATTACK!

If you ever find yourself facing off against a vampire, don't worry—there are many ways to stay safe!

VAMPIRE 101

Crucifix.

Stay calm and keep your distance. Vampires rely on fear to overpower you. Keeping a cool head is your first defense.

Hold up a crucifix. Vampires are repelled by holy symbols, so if you have one, use it to keep them at bay.

EXPERT SURVIVAL TIPS

Keep a wooden stake. If you need to defend yourself, a stake through the heart will stop a vampire for good.

Carry holy water. A few drops can cause a vampire to retreat, buying you time to escape.

"There are only two kinds of vampire hunters: good ones and dead ones."

Laurell K. Hamilton, *Circus of the Damned*

EXPERT SURVIVAL TIPS

Stay in well-lit areas. Vampires thrive in the shadows, so stick to places with bright lights or wait for the sunrise.

Know the signs. Look for pale skin, sharp fangs, and no reflection in mirrors—classic vampire traits!

Shine a bright light on them. Vampires dislike sunlight and strong lights. A flashlight or even your phone's torch can help to slow them down.

Use garlic as a shield. Vampires can't stand the smell of garlic. A clove of garlic around your neck or in your pocket is an easy way to protect yourself.

Keep them out. Vampires can't enter your home unless they're invited, so never let a stranger in after dark without being sure of who they are!

SURVIVING A WEREWOLF ATTACK!

Facing a werewolf can be terrifying, but don't howl with fear just yet! With the right strategies, you can survive the encounter and keep your inner adventurer intact. Here's how to handle this hair-raising situation...

WEREWOLF 101

Do not try to run from a werewolf!

Stay calm and do not run. Like any predator, a werewolf will see running as a challenge. Stay still and assess your options.

Avoid provoking the werewolf. Do not yell, throw things, or make sudden movements. Werewolves are aggressive and provoking them could trigger an attack!

EXPERT SURVIVAL TIP

Avoid exploring the wilderness during a full moon. Werewolves transform during a full moon, so it's best to stay indoors, or in well-lit, populated areas.

"Werewolves were far more terrifying than vampires. It is probably the idea of seeing the human within the beast and knowing you can't reach it. It might as well be a great white shark."

Glen Duncan

Werewolves rarely travel alone. A pack of werewolves is a terrifying sight!

EXPERT WEREWOLF SURVIVAL TIPS

Know the signs of werewolf activity. Look for large claw marks, strange howling, and paw prints larger than any wolf's.

Protect your scent. Werewolves have an incredible sense of smell. Use mud or masking scents to make it harder for them to track you.

Silver dagger.

Defend yourself with silver. Werewolves are famously vulnerable to silver. If you have any silver jewelry, coins, or tools, use them to battle the beast.

Find a barrier. Werewolves are powerful, but they can't break through everything! Climb a sturdy tree, get inside a building, or find a body of water (werewolves aren't known for their swimming skills).

Wait it out. Most werewolves return to their human form by sunrise. If you can stay safe until dawn, you might be able to escape without further danger.

SURVIVING AN ALIEN INVASION!

If Earth ever faces an alien invasion, staying calm, informed, and resourceful will be key to survival. Whether they're here to conquer or just visiting, it's time to channel your inner sci-fi hero and follow these survival steps.

ALIEN 101

Stay hidden. Aliens might be technologically advanced, so avoiding detection is your first priority. Seek shelter underground, in dense forests, or in areas with low visibility.

EXPERT SURVIVAL TIPS

Know your defenses. Common sci-fi wisdom suggests that aliens might have weaknesses to Earth's natural elements, like germs, water, or gravity. Learn as much as you can about their vulnerabilities.

Use camouflage. If aliens rely on heat vision or advanced scanning, covering yourself with materials that mask your heat signature, like mud or thermal blankets, can help.

EXPERT SURVIVAL TIPS

Be cautious about communication. If you encounter an alien, avoid aggressive actions and proceed carefully. Try universal signs of peace, like open palms or non-threatening gestures, but be ready to run if needed!

Form alliances with people. It's true there is strength in numbers! Work with others to create a plan for defense, resource sharing, and escape if necessary.

Avoid technology. Advanced aliens could track communications or electrical signals, so turn off phones, radios, and other devices to stay off their radar.

Gather supplies. Stock up on food, water, and essentials for long-term survival. Keep your gear portable in case you need to move quickly.

Watch the skies. Pay attention to spacecraft movements. If they're attacking specific areas, move away from high-priority targets like cities, military bases, and power plants.

Stay informed. Listen to emergency broadcasts or trusted news sources to understand the situation and follow any evacuation orders.

SURVIVING IN A HAUNTED HOUSE!

Staying safe in a haunted house is all about keeping your cool, being prepared, and knowing how to handle the spooky situations that might come your way. Whether it's ghosts, creepy noises, or objects that move on their own, here's how to survive and make it out unscathed...

POLTERGEIST 101

Stick together. Never split up—ghosts and ghouls thrive on isolating their targets. Stick with your group and keep each other in sight.

Carry a flashlight. Haunted houses are often dark and shadowy places. A good flashlight helps you to see ahead and avoid tripping over something spooky.

EXPERT SURVIVAL TIPS

Watch out for spooky signs. Flickering lights, footsteps, or objects moving on their own are clues that a spirit might be near—proceed cautiously.

Keep your exit strategy in mind. Know where the doors, windows, and escape routes are at all times.

EXPERT SURVIVAL TIPS

Bring protective items. Salt, sage, or holy water are traditional tools for warding off spirits. Draw a salt circle for temporary protection if needed.

Be aware of cold spots. Sudden drops in temperature can indicate ghostly activity, so stay alert and move carefully.

Avoid mirrors and reflective surfaces. They are often linked to paranormal activity and can be unsettling.

Sage.

Don't engage with the supernatural. If you hear a voice calling your name, or see a mysterious figure, don't follow it!

Respect the spirits. Haunted houses often have a tragic backstory. Avoid provoking spirits by touching objects, making loud noises, or being disrespectful.

Escape! If things get too intense, look for the nearest exit. No one will judge you for leaving a haunted house—they'll be impressed you entered in the first place!

SURVIVING A ZOMBIE APOCALYPSE!

If the undead ever start roaming the streets, don't panic—you've got this! Surviving a zombie apocalypse is about staying calm, being prepared, and outsmarting the living dead.

GET SOMEWHERE SAFE

Find shelter. Look for an empty building that is strong and secure, with few entrances.

Block the entrances. Use furniture or anything heavy to block the doors and windows. Zombies are strong, but not clever!

Stay quiet. Zombies are drawn to noise, so keep things as quiet as possible.

»

STOCK UP ON SUPPLIES

Food and water. Collect enough non-perishable food and bottled water to last a few days...or weeks!

First-aid kit. Keep bandages, antiseptic wipes, painkillers, and medicines in case of injuries.

Tools and weapons. Grab things like a flashlight, a sturdy stick, or even a baseball bat to defend yourself against zombies, if needed.

AVOID THE ZOMBIES

Stay out of sight. Zombies aren't great at finding people who stay hidden. Move quietly, find places to hide, and avoid drawing the zombies' attention.

Travel during the day. Zombies might be slower or easier to spot in daylight. Avoid exploring at night. You don't want to be surprised in the dark!

Know their weaknesses. Zombies can't handle damage to their heads. If you have to defend yourself, aim there!

EXPERT SURVIVAL TIP

Find a group. Survival is easier with friends. Team up with people you trust so you can watch each other's backs.

LONG-TERM SURVIVAL

Find a safe zone. Keep an ear out for news about safe zones that zombies haven't reached yet.

Grow your own food. If the apocalypse lasts a while, plant seeds to grow fruits and vegetables.

Plan for an escape. Always have a backup plan to move on if zombies find your hideout.

By staying smart, prepared, and calm, you'll be ready to survive even the scariest zombie invasion. Who knows—you might even become the leader of the human resistance.

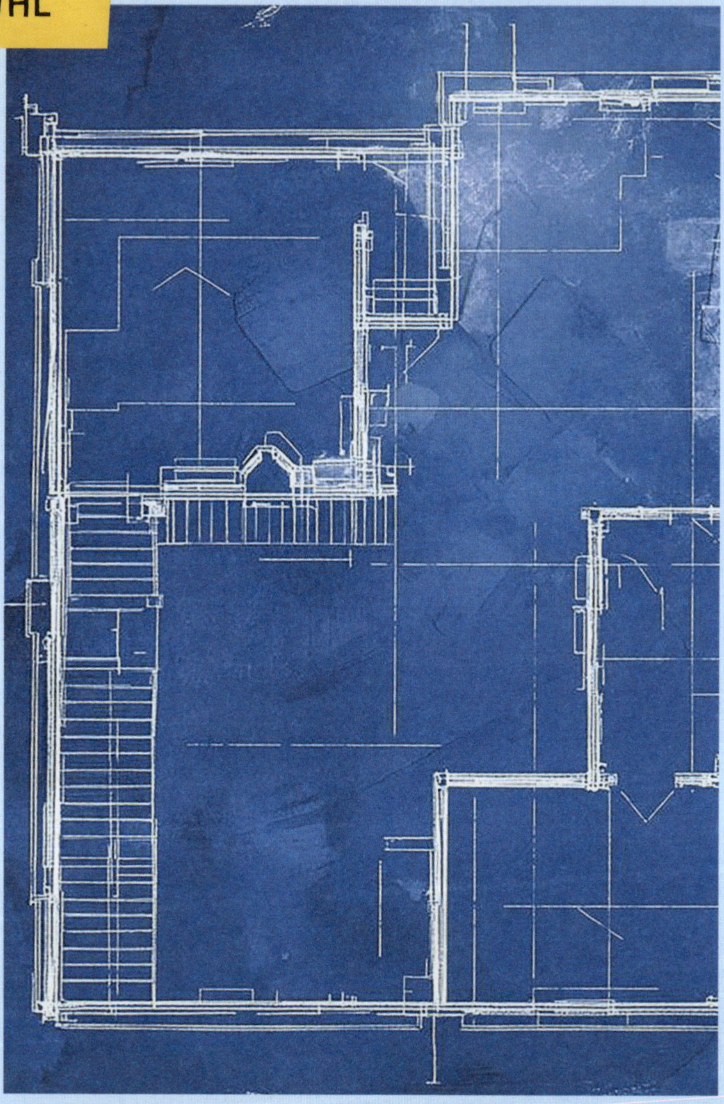

EXPERT SURVIVAL TIP

Zombies can't swim, so a boat would be a great way to stay safe near water.

SURVIVING A DRAGON ENCOUNTER!

Dragons may only exist in stories and legends, but if you ever did find yourself face-to-face with one, you'd need to stay sharp in order to survive!

STAY CALM

Dragons are highly perceptive and can sense fear. Keeping your cool might earn you some respect.

KNOW YOUR DRAGONS

FIRE-BREATHING DRAGONS

Keep your distance! Stay behind rocks, trees, or anything that could shield you from their flames.

ICE DRAGONS

Bundle up. These dragons can freeze you in your tracks. Look for warm spots or use heat-resistant gear.

WATER DRAGONS

Avoid getting near lakes or rivers where they might ambush you. If you're in water, swim to the shore.

PEACE NOT WAR!

Speak calmly. Dragons are often portrayed as intelligent. Use a confident, respectful tone when speaking to them.

Offer a gift. Dragons love shiny objects and hoards of treasure. If you have anything reflective or valuable, give it to them as a peace offering.

Avoid threats. Don't make sudden movements or draw your weapons.

ESCAPE

Distract the dragon. Throw a shiny object to divert its attention before trying to escape.

Back away. If the dragon isn't attacking you, back away slowly without turning your back.

Use terrain to your advantage. Dragons are enormous, so hide in tight spaces, caves, or under dense cover so they can't follow you.

DEFEND YOURSELF (ONLY IF YOU HAVE TO)

Aim for weak spots. In most stories, dragons' weak spots are their underbellies or eyes. Check for missing scales, too.

Avoid combat at all costs. Dragons can fly, breathe fire or ice, and are incredibly strong, so direct combat should only be a last resort.

FINAL ADVICE

Dragons are as unpredictable as they are magnificent. Whether they're guarding a hoard of treasure, protecting their territory, or simply flying by, surviving an encounter will depend on staying calm, thinking smart, and getting a little lucky!

DRAGON SURVIVAL KIT

- **A mirror** to reflect fire or dazzle a dragon with its own reflection
- **A shield or cloak** to protect against fire or ice
- **Shiny objects** to give to the dragon as gifts

PICTURE CREDITS

Geoff Ball: 50, 51, 56, 57, 58, 59, 60, 73, 74.

Matt Denny: 1, 8, 10, 18, 24, 25, 45, 53, 65, 66, 68, 75, 76, 77, 83, 121, 123, 126, 138

Malgorzata Detner: 105, 106, 109, 110, 113

Freepik: 4, 5, 9, 11, 13, 14, 15, 16, 17, 19, 20, 21, 22, 23, 25, 34, 35, 36, 41, 42, 44, 45, 47, 48, 49, 50, 52, 54, 55, 64, 65, 67, 70, 71, 72, 73, 74, 76, 79, 84, 93, 94, 95, 97, 99, 102, 103, 104, 105, 110, 117, 134

Noah James (CGI Illustrations and Photographs): 4, 5, 6, 7, 10, 26, 32, 33, 35, 46, 56, 57, 61, 62, 68, 69, 78, 81, 82, 85, 86, 87, 88, 89, 90, 92, 100, 101, 107, 108, 111, 112, 104, 105, 106, 119, 120, 122, 124, 125, 127, 128, 129, 130, 131, 132, 133, 134, 135, 136, 137, 139, 140, 141, 142

Matt O'Neil: 85, 86, 87, 91, 92, 95, 96, 98, 99

Public Domain image: 39 (Popular Science Magazine, 1873)

Ben Sharman: 28, 30, 143

Peter Wilks: 27, 33